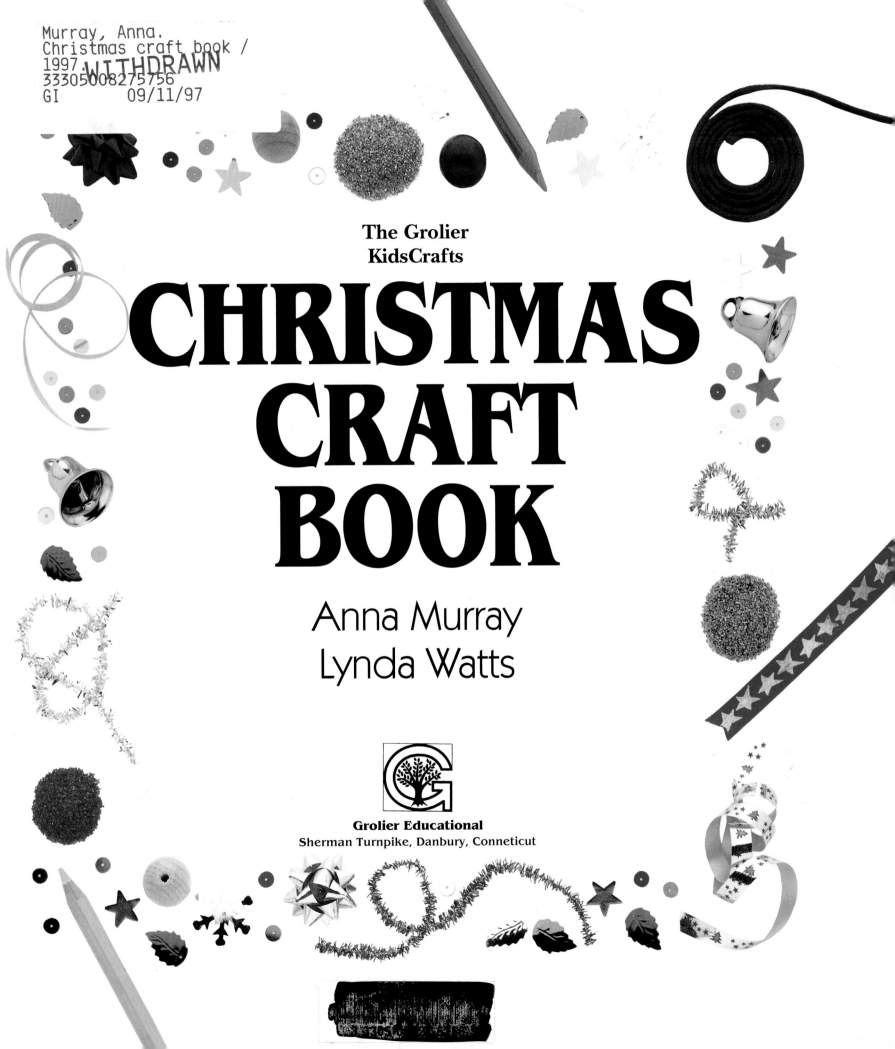

The Grolier
KidsCrafts

CHRISTMAS CRAFT BOOK

Anna Murray
Lynda Watts

Grolier Educational
Sherman Turnpike, Danbury, Conneticut

Published 1997 by Grolier Educational
Sherman Turnpike
Danbury, CT 06816

© 1992 Salamander Books Ltd.

Set ISBN: 0-7172-9090-5
Volume ISBN: 0-7172-9093-X

For information address the publisher:
Grolier Educational, Sherman Turnpike, Danbury, CT 06816

Library of Congress Cataloging-in-Publication Data

Murray, Anna.
  [My Christmas craft book]
  The Grolier kidscrafts Christmas craft book / Anna Murray, Lynda Watts.
    p.   cm.
  Originally published in 1993 under the title: My Christmas craft book.
  Includes index.
  Summary: Provides patterns and instructions for creating a variety of Christmas
decorations and small gift items.
  ISBN 0-7172-9093-X (hardcover)
  1. Christmas decorations—Juvenile literature.   2. Handicraft—Juvenile
literature   [1. Christmas decorations.   2. Handicraft.]   I. Watts, Lynda.
II. Grolier Educational (Firm)   III. Title.
TT900.C4M8698   1997
745.5942—dc21

                                                                        97-5690
                                                                          CIP
                                                                           AC

CREDITS
Commissioning editor: Veronica Ross
Art Director: Rachael Stone
Photographer: Jonathan Pollock
Assistant photographer: Peter Cassidy
Additional designs by: Cheryl Owen
Editor: Helen Stone
Designer: Cherry Randell
Illustrator: John Hutchinson
Character illustrator: Jo Gapper
Diagram artist: Malcolm Porter
Typeset by: SX Composing DTP, Essex
Color separation by: Regent Publishing Services, Ltd., Hong Kong
Printed in USA

CONTENTS

INTRODUCTION

The weeks leading up to Christmas are some of the most exciting of the year, with so much to plan and prepare. In the *Christmas Craft Book* we show you how to make almost everything you will need to make your Christmas really special. There are lots of decorations to make plus party hats, mobiles, and more. We also show you how to make tempting goodies to eat and a range of fun ideas to give as presents.

BEFORE YOU BEGIN

- Check with an adult before you begin any project.
- Read the instructions first.
- Gather together all the items you need before you begin.
- When using glue or paints, cover your work surface with newspaper or an old cloth.
- Protect your clothes with an apron or wear very old clothes.

WHEN YOU HAVE FINISHED

- Put everything away. Store special pens, paints, glue, etc. in old ice-cream containers or coffee cans.
- Wash paintbrushes and remember to put the tops back on pens, paints, and glue containers.
- If you are baking, put away all the ingredients, wash any dishes, and leave the kitchen clean.

SAFETY FIRST!

You will be able to make most of the projects yourself, but sometimes you will need help. Look out for the SAFETY TIP. It appears on those projects where you will need to ask an adult for help. Remember to use your common sense when using anything hot or sharp and, if in any doubt, ask an adult for advice.

Please remember the basic rules of safety:

- Never leave scissors open or lying around where smaller children can reach them.
- Always stick needles and pins into a pin cushion or a scrap of cloth when you are not using them.
- Never use an oven or a sharp knife without the help or supervision of an adult.

Get everything ready before you start, and don't forget to clean up afterward!

Be very careful when using sharp scissors.

EQUIPMENT & INGREDIENTS

Every project will list all the things you need. Many designs use glitter, shiny paper, or tinsel; look among last year's Christmas decorations before buying new materials. Candies and cookies will require baking ingredients. You will probably find most of the ingredients you need in the kitchen cupboard, but check with an adult before taking anything. Some items, such as jewelry fittings or special baking molds, will need to be bought at large stores or specialty shops.

USING PATTERNS

At the back of the book you will find the patterns you will need to make some of the projects in the book. Using a pencil, trace the pattern you need onto tracing paper. If you are making a project with fabric, cut the pattern out and pin it onto the fabric. Cut out the shape. If you want to cut the pattern out of cardboard, turn your tracing over and rub firmly over the pattern outline with a pencil. The pattern will transfer on to the board. Cut out this shape.

Once you have gained confidence making some of the projects in this book, go on to adapt the ideas to create some of your own designs.

GROWN UPS TAKE NOTE

Every project in the *Christmas Craft Book* has been designed with simplicity, yet effectiveness, in mind. However, some potentially dangerous items such as an oven or a sharp knife are used for some projects. Your involvement will depend on the ability of the child, but we recommend that you read through any project before it is undertaken.

Make sure an adult helps you when you are cooking.

ADVENT CALENDAR

Advent calendars are designed to contain a message or a small gift, which you open on each of the 24 days leading up to Christmas – so you will need to make this calendar well in advance. To celebrate Christmas Eve, you could make the gift inside the last matchbox extra special.

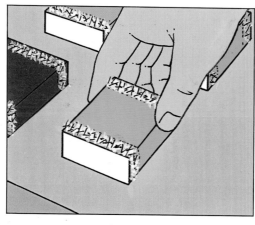

1 Cut the foil into strips the same width as the matchboxes and long enough to wrap around them. Coat the foil with glue and wrap it around the matchbox. Glue tinsel around each end of the matchbox.

2 Position the matchboxes on the gold board, so they are in six rows. Glue them in place. Put some books on top of the matchboxes to weight them. Let them dry.

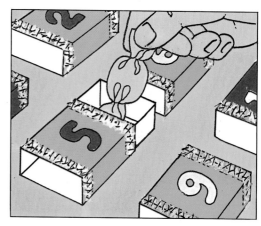

YOU WILL NEED

18½ inch × 16 inch gold mounting board
24 empty matchboxes
Colored foil paper
Glitter pens
Fine tinsel and paper ribbon
All-purpose glue
24 candies or small gifts

3 Using the glitter pens, draw the numbers 1 to 24 on the boxes. Cut two holly leaves from green foil and berries from red foil, and glue them to the top of the calendar.

4 Glue some paper ribbon around the outer edges of the gold board. Glue a loop of tinsel to the top. Put a candy or small gift inside each of the boxes.

CHRISTMAS STOCKING

This Christmas, make a special stocking to put beside the fire, or use it as a novelty bag for small presents. Use a glue stick for this project, as any of the wetter glues may make the color run in the crêpe paper.

YOU WILL NEED

Double-sided crêpe paper
Thick sewing thread and
    needle
Tracing paper and pencil
Scraps of white, black,
    and colored cardboard
Scissors
Pins
Glue stick and pen

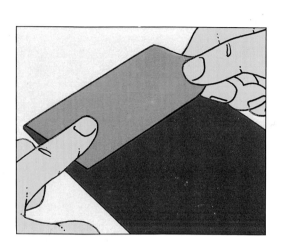

1 Using a pencil, trace the stocking pattern on page 42. Cut out the pattern and pin it to a piece of crêpe paper which has been folded in half. Carefully cut around the pattern to make two stocking shapes. Fold down the top of the stockings to show the second color of crêpe paper.

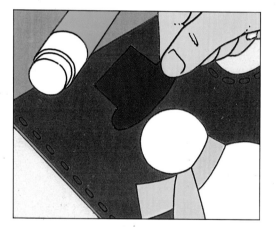

3 Cut a snowman shape from white paper and stick it in place on the stocking. Cut a hat from black paper and a scarf from a different color. Glue them onto the snowman.

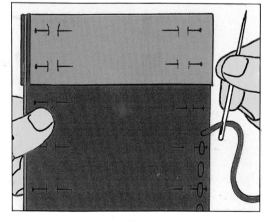

2 Pin the stockings together and, using the needle and thread, sew around the outer edge, as shown above.

4 Cut a small carrot shape for the nose and circles for buttons and glue them on. Trim the hat with some holly leaves cut from green paper and berries from red. Draw dots for the eyes with the pen.

SHINY CANDY SWAG

Make a decorative candy swag from a selection of wrapped candy, some tinsel, and ribbon. Easy to make, this fun idea also provides a tasty treat when you take down your Christmas decorations – if you can wait that long!

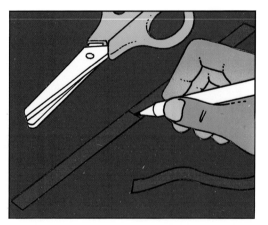

2 Staple one end of each candy to the ribbon. Leave a 2 inch gap either side of the pen mark for the center loop.

1 Cut a piece of ribbon the length you want your finished swag to be. Mark the halfway point with a pen to show where to position the center loop.

YOU WILL NEED
1 inch wide ribbon
Tinsel
Wrapped candies
Stapler
Shiny giftwrap ribbon
Scissors
Cardboard
Pen

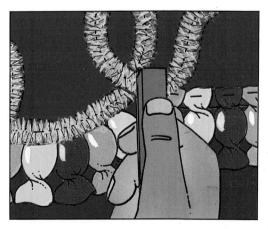

3 Make a tinsel loop, and staple to one end of the swag. Staple a long length of tinsel to the ribbon to cover the stapled ends of the candies. Make a tinsel loop at the gap in the middle of the ribbon. Continue to staple the tinsel to the ribbon until you reach the other end. Finish with another tinsel loop.

4 Tie the giftwrap ribbon to each end of the swag and make a bow around the central loop. Pull the scissor blades along the length of the trailing ends of giftwrap ribbon to make them curl up.

5 To make the rosette decoration, cut out a circle of board. Staple tinsel around the edge of the board, leaving a loop at the top. Staple candies and shiny ribbon to the center of the card.

POP-UP SANTA

Cards that have a pop-up section are expensive to buy, but not that hard to make. Try making several cards so that you can give one to each friend. Make sure you use cardboard and paper that is firm and not floppy.

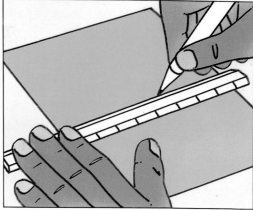

1 On the blue cardboard, draw a rectangle 11 inches × 7 inches. Draw a line down the center to divide it into two. Cut out the cardboard and fold it in half.

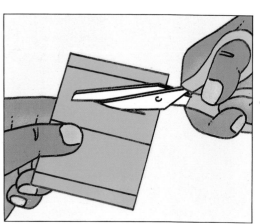

2 Trace the patterns on page 43. Turn the tracings over and lay the body pattern onto red paper, the beard onto white paper, the sack onto brown paper, and the chimney onto green. Rub over the outlines with a pencil. The images will appear on the colored paper. Cut out the patterns and the slot in the chimney.

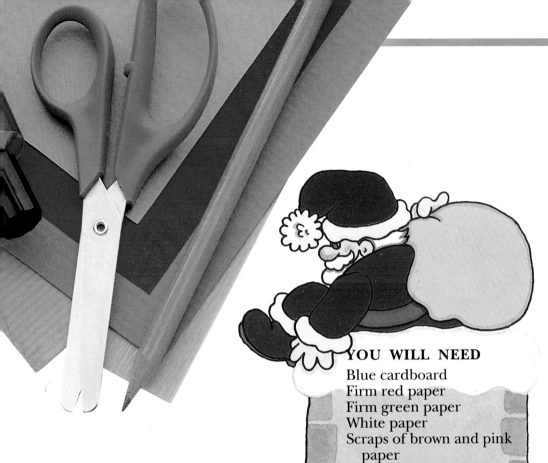

YOU WILL NEED
Blue cardboard
Firm red paper
Firm green paper
White paper
Scraps of brown and pink
 paper
Scissors and ruler
All-purpose glue
Black felt-tip pen
Tracing paper and pencil

5 Fold the chimney into shape as shown, and slip the Santa into the slot. Fold a little of Santa's body down and stick it to the inside of the chimney.

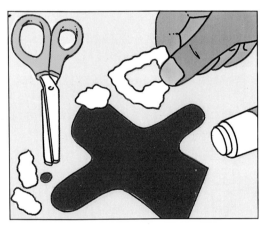

3 Using the body pattern as a guide, cut two cuffs and a pompon from white paper and a face from pink paper. Glue all the shapes onto the body shape. Draw on the eyes and add a red nose.

4 To make the roof, draw a rectangle 5½ inches × 7 inches onto green paper and cut it out. Stick it to one half of the inside of the card. Cut some extra white paper to look like snow, and glue one piece to the front of the chimney and one to the edge of the green roof.

6 Position the chimney and Santa inside the card, as shown. This is how it will look when the card is open. Dab glue on the chimney's tabs, then stick it in place.

GIFT SOAPS

Make a small present look really special by taking extra time and effort to wrap it. Miniature soaps look lovely wrapped in two layers of brightly colored net and secured with a pretty bow.

YOU WILL NEED

Miniature soaps
  or bath balls
Net in two colors
Ribbon
Scissors
Two plates – one slightly
  smaller than the other
Small rubber bands
Ball-point pen

1 Take a piece of net in each color. Lay the large plate onto one piece of net and the smaller plate onto the other. Draw around both plates with a pen and cut out the two circles.

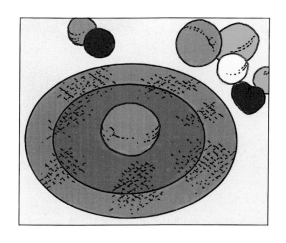

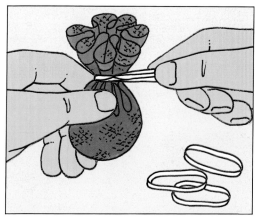

4 Decorate the soap bags with a matching ribbon, making sure you cover the rubber band. Tie into a bow at the front.

3 Bunch both circles of net up around the soap. Secure in place with a small rubber band. Pull the net around a little to make an attractive frill.

2 Place the larger circle of net on top of the smaller circle. Put a single soap or a few bath balls in the center of the net circles.

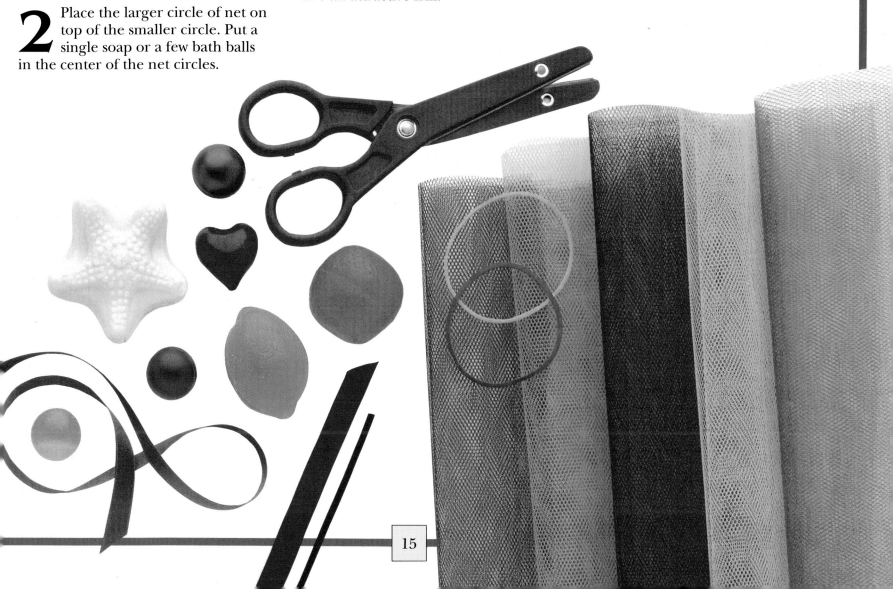

FLYING ANGELS

Hang this cute mobile in a doorway or from the corner of a room. If you don't want to make a complete mobile, the individual angels can be used as Christmas tree ornaments.

1 Using a pencil, trace the dress pattern on page 44. Cut out the pattern and pin it to the crêpe paper. Cut out the dress, then fold it in half along the foldline and cut away the neck hole. Fold the tabs back and glue them down. Glue the edges of the sleeves together.

2 Thread the needle with gold yarn and sew around the neck opening, leaving long ends of thread.

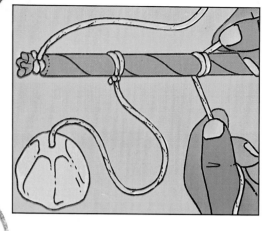

3 Paint a face on a large bead. Cut the gold yarn into pieces about ¾ inch long and glue them to the head for hair.

6 Wrap ribbon around the stick and glue the ends in place. Cut the gold cord into four lengths. Tie one piece to the ends of the stick, so that the mobile can hang up. Make three gold bells following the instructions given for Bell Pendant on pages 26 and 27. Tie each bell onto a length of cord, then tie the bells onto the stick. Hang the angels by folding their pipe cleaner hands over the cord.

4 For the body, cut a pipe cleaner in half and twist the two pieces together as shown. Dab glue onto the ends of the arms and push on the small beads. Dab glue onto the neck and push on the head. Put the dress onto the body. Pull the thread ends tightly around the neck and tie them into a bow.

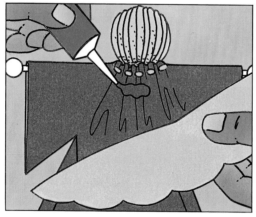

5 Using a pencil, trace the wing pattern on page 44. Turn the tracing paper over and lay it on the back of the gold board. Rub firmly over the outline with a pencil. The pattern will appear on the board. Cut out one wing. Now lay the shape back on the gold board. Draw around it and cut out another wing shape. Glue the shapes together and stick them on the back of the angel. Make three angels in this way.

YOU WILL NEED
Crêpe paper
3 large white beads
6 small white beads
3 pipe cleaners
Gold yarn and needle
Gold cardboard
Stick, 1 foot long
1 yard of ribbon
1½ yards of gold cord
All-purpose glue and scissors
Poster paints and paintbrush

RIBBON ROSETTES

These ribbon rosettes are very quick and easy to make yet give a really stylish finish to your Christmas presents. Try tying your parcels with shiny, metallic ribbon and making a matching rosette for the top.

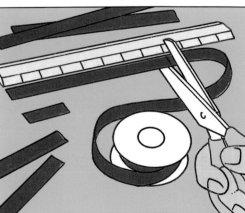

YOU WILL NEED

Shiny giftwrap ribbon
Double-sided tape
Scissors
Ruler

1 Cut eight lengths of ribbon 8 inches long. Cut a small piece of ribbon 2 inches long, for the central loop.

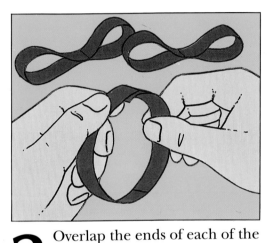

4 To make a two-color bow, cut four pieces each of two different colored ribbons. Make eight bow loops as in step 2. Criss-cross the loops, using first one color then another, before finishing with a small center loop.

2 Overlap the ends of each of the long lengths of ribbon and stick together with double-sided tape to form a loop. Fasten each loop in the middle, using tape on the inside of the loop as shown.

3 Tape the loops together by placing each one diagonally on top of the one below, to form a criss-cross pattern. To finish, tape the ends of the short piece of ribbon together to form a tiny loop. Tape this neatly in the center of the rosette.

3-D GIFT TAGS

Add a special touch to Christmas parcels by matching the gift tag to the paper. When making 3-D gift tags, it is best to choose wrapping paper with a repeat pattern that has a clear outline to cut around.

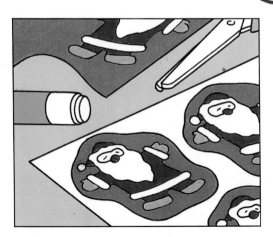

1 Roughly cut out four identical motifs from the giftwrap. Glue the motifs to a sheet of paper to make them stiffer.

2 Now, carefully cut around three of the motifs following the outline of the shape. From the fourth motif, cut out separate features, such as Santa's face.

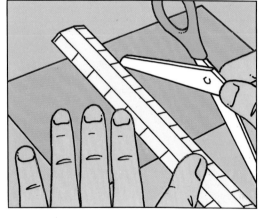

3 Cut a piece of cardboard slightly taller than your chosen motif and at least twice as wide. Score down the center of the board with a ruler and scissors to make a fold line.

SAFETY TIP: *Make sure an adult helps you when using sharp scissors.*

YOU WILL NEED
Colored cardboard
Giftwrap with
  repeat pattern
Scissors
Glue stick
Plain paper
Ruler
Double-sided sticky pads
Hole punch

5 Fix the smaller sections from the fourth motif in the appropriate places using the sticky pads to create a 3-D effect. Fold the board in half and punch a hole in the top left-hand corner. Thread with ribbon.

4 Turn the card over and glue the first motif to the right-hand side. Position sticky pads all over the motif. Put the second motif on top of the first so that it sticks to the pads. Repeat for the third motif.

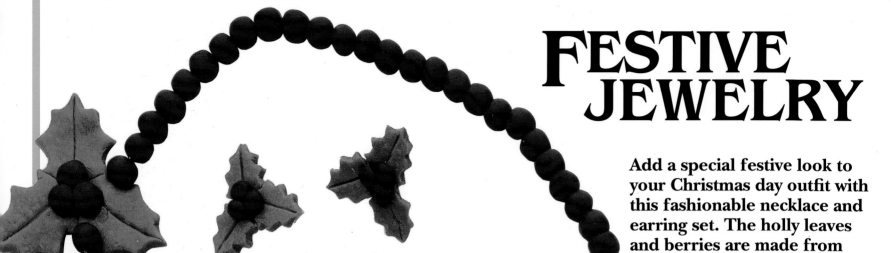

FESTIVE JEWELRY

Add a special festive look to your Christmas day outfit with this fashionable necklace and earring set. The holly leaves and berries are made from colored modeling clay that is baked in the oven.

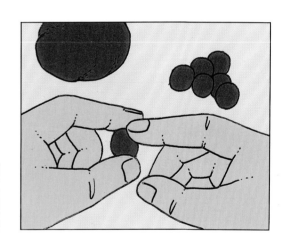

3 Roll some red modeling clay in your hands to make small balls to use as berries for the necklace and the earrings.

2 Roll out some green modeling clay onto a smooth surface. Press the holly pattern into the clay and cut around it. Cut out three clusters of leaves.

1 Draw a cluster of three holly leaves onto some cardboard. Cut the shape out and use it as a pattern for your jewelry.

SAFETY TIP: *Make sure an adult helps you when using the oven.*

22

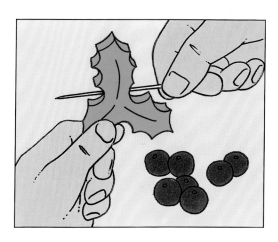

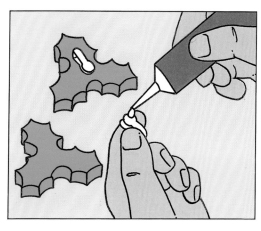

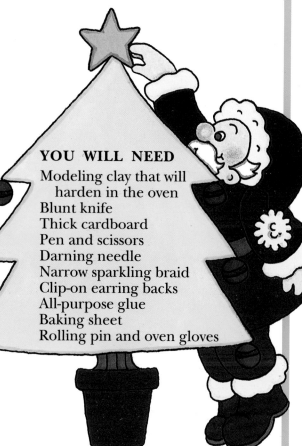

YOU WILL NEED

Modeling clay that will
    harden in the oven
Blunt knife
Thick cardboard
Pen and scissors
Darning needle
Narrow sparkling braid
Clip-on earring backs
All-purpose glue
Baking sheet
Rolling pin and oven gloves

4 To make the necklace, carefully push the darning needle through one leaf from one edge to the other. Press three berries into the center of the cluster. Push the darning needle through the center of the remaining berries. For the earrings, draw a small cluster of holly leaves onto card and cut two earring shapes from clay. Decorate with berries.

5 Bake the shapes in the oven following the instructions on the package. Wearing oven gloves, remove the shapes from the oven and leave to cool before making up the jewelry. For the necklace, thread the berries and the leaves onto the braid and knot the ends. For the earrings, glue clip-on earring backs to the back of the leaves.

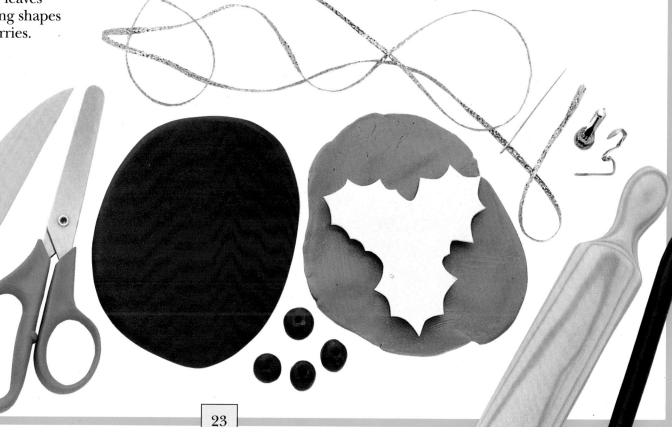

CHRISTMAS ANGEL

Put this enchanting angel on the top of your Christmas tree as a very special decoration. Her skirt is made from soft pink feathers, but you could give her a white feather skirt if you prefer.

YOU WILL NEED

1 yard marabou feather trim
White and gold cardboard
A 2 inch white bead
All-purpose glue
Poster paints and paintbrush
Curling gold paper ribbon
A pipe cleaner
2 gold doilies
Wooden skewer
Cotton wool and ribbon
Masking tape and scissors

1 Trace the cone and hand patterns on page 43. Turn the tracings over and lay onto white board. Rub over the outlines with a pencil. The patterns will appear on the board; cut out. Now cut out a second hand shape. Punch holes into the cone for the arms (see pattern). Roll the cone into shape and tape the joint.

2 Starting at the bottom, wrap the feather trim around the cone. Use small dabs of glue to hold it in place. To make the collar, cut a section from one of the doilies and glue it around the top of the cone.

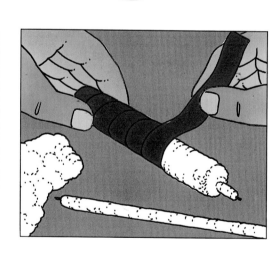

3 Paint a face on the bead. Dribble some glue into the hole in the bead and push in the skewer. Glue lengths of curling ribbon onto the bead for hair.

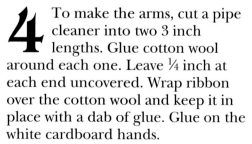

4 To make the arms, cut a pipe cleaner into two 3 inch lengths. Glue cotton wool around each one. Leave ¼ inch at each end uncovered. Wrap ribbon over the cotton wool and keep it in place with a dab of glue. Glue on the white cardboard hands.

5 Push the arms into the holes in the cone. Push the head into the cone. From the gold board, cut a small square for the book and a circle for the halo. Fold the book in half and glue the hands to each side of it. Fold the doily in half and glue to the angel for wings.

BELL PENDANT

Empty egg cartons can be cut up to make great bell shapes. Decorate the bell-shaped pieces of carton with shiny foil and tinsel, group them together and make an attractive bell pendant to hang from the wall or ceiling.

YOU WILL NEED

Plastic egg carton
Gold or silver foil
Very fine tinsel
Small bells
Cardboard
Darning needle
Scissors
Tape

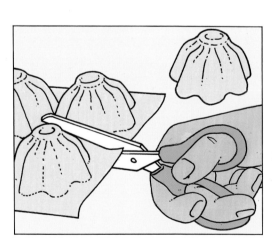

1 Carefully cut out the raised sections of the egg carton using scissors.

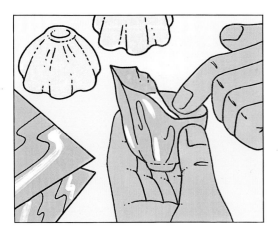

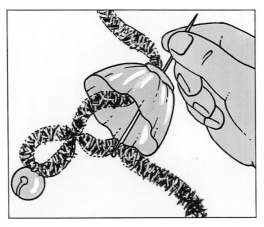

2 Cover the carton pieces with gold or silver foil. Make sure you smooth the foil over the surface and tuck the ends inside the shapes to secure them. If necessary, hold any loose edges in place with tape (not glue) on the inside.

3 Thread the needle with tinsel. Push the needle down through the top of the carton, taking care not to tear the foil. Thread the small bell onto the tinsel. Now take the tinsel back up through the hole in the top of the carton. Knot the pieces of tinsel together inside the carton, about 1 inch above the bell. Repeat to make three bell shapes.

4 To make the ring, draw two circles, one inside the other, onto board. Cut the ring out and wrap tinsel around it as you would to make pompons.

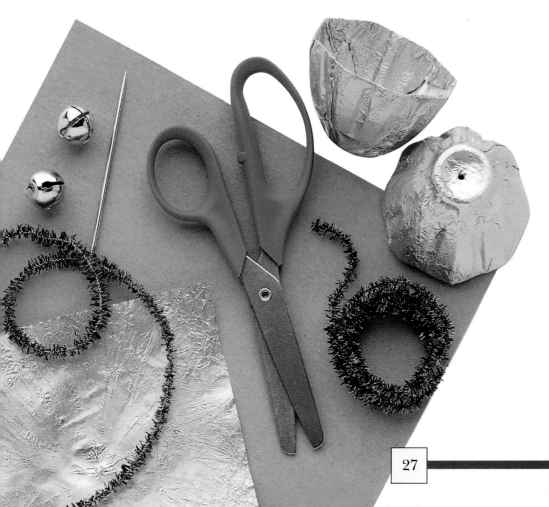

5 Hang the bells on the ring by threading the hanging tinsel through the layers wrapped around the ring. Make sure each bell hangs from a slightly different length. Cut off any loose ends.

REINDEER HAT

Give everyone a smile at Christmas with this jolly reindeer party hat. Make your hat as glamorous as you can by adding lots of shiny ribbon, glitter, and beads.

YOU WILL NEED

Green and beige cardboard
3 yellow pipe cleaners
Wooden bead
Red glitter
Black felt-tip pen
2 bells
Giftwrapping ribbon
Strings of beads
All-purpose glue
Tracing paper and pencil
Scissors

1 Cut a strip of green cardboard 3¼ inches wide and long enough to go around your head. Overlap the ends and glue together. Glue giftwrapping ribbon and beads in loops around the hat.

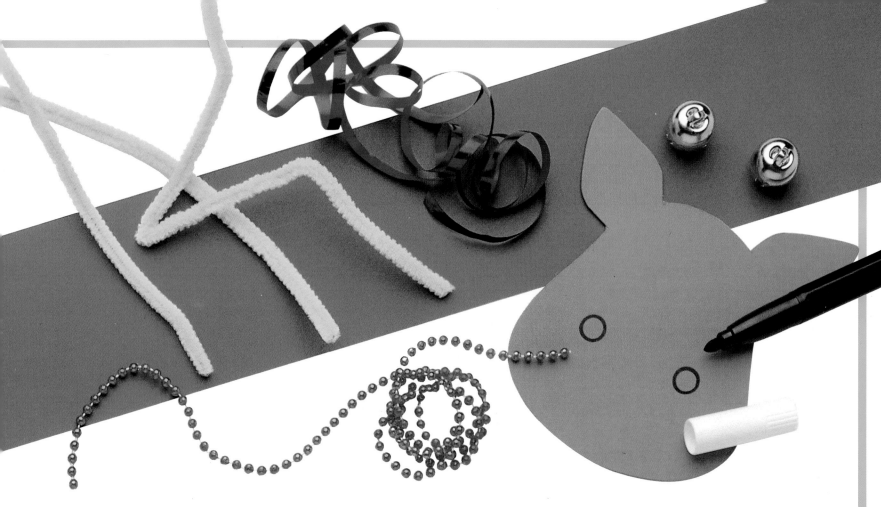

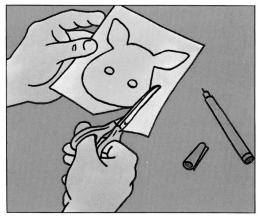

2 Using a pencil, trace the reindeer face on page 46. Turn the tracing paper over and lay it on the beige board. Rub firmly over the outline with a pencil. The image will appear on the board. Cut out the face. Draw the eyes with a felt-tip pen.

3 Cover the bead with glue and sprinkle it with glitter. Let it dry and then glue it to the reindeer's face. To make the antlers, bend the pipe cleaners in half and glue them behind the head as shown.

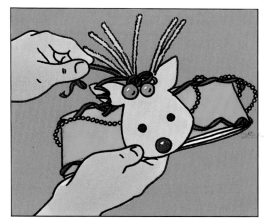

4 Glue the reindeer face to the green board strip. Tie the bells onto some ribbon and tie these around the antlers so that they rest between the reindeer's ears. Bend the pipe cleaners over slightly to give the antlers some shape.

ICED COOKIES

These delicious iced cookies are great fun to make. Decorate them with icing, and cake decorations like candied cherries and pineapple.

1 Turn the oven on to 325°F/ 180°C. Wash your hands well. Put the flour and the cinnamon into a mixing bowl. Break the butter into little pieces and, using your fingers, rub it into the flour until it forms little balls.

2 Add the sugar and the egg to the mixture and mix well until it forms a thick dough. Sprinkle a clean surface with a little flour and roll out the dough with a rolling pin. Grease a baking tray with a little butter. Using cookie cutters, cut the dough into different shapes.

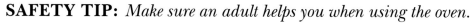

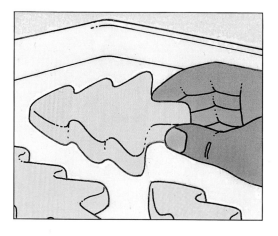

SAFETY TIP: *Make sure an adult helps you when using the oven.*

3 Carefully lift the shapes onto a baking tray. Bake the cookies for about 15 minutes or until the edges turn golden. Wearing oven gloves, remove them from the oven and let them cool on a wire rack.

4 To make the icing, mix the powdered sugar with 3 teaspoons of water; the icing should form a thick, smooth paste. Add a few drops of food coloring to the icing to tint it slightly.

YOU WILL NEED
- 6 ounces plain flour
- 2 teaspoons ground cinnamon
- 4 ounces butter
- 1½ ounces brown sugar
- 1 egg
- 4 ounces powdered sugar
- Food coloring

5 Place the cookies on a clean, flat plate and dribble the icing over them, letting it run down the sides of the cookies. When it has just started to set, gently press on the chopped candied cherries and pineapple. Let the icing set.

MR. FROST

Make a jolly Mr. Frosty snowman using scraps of felt for a Christmas tree decoration that can be used year after year. Simple to make, yet very effective, this idea can easily be adapted to make angels or Santas.

YOU WILL NEED
White, black, and orange felt
Thin cardboard
Firm black cardboard
Large white wooden bead
Red ribbon
Black felt-tip pen
Needle and thread
Cotton
All-purpose glue
Scissors and saucer

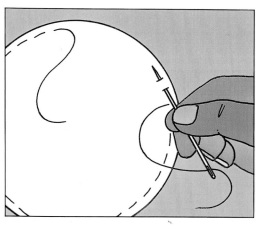

1 Lay a saucer onto some white felt, draw around it with a pen, and cut out. Sew around the edge of the circle as shown. Pull the ends of the thread to draw the felt into a ball shape. Leave a gap in the top and the threads hanging.

4 For the hat, glue some black felt onto a piece of black board. Cut out a circle and make a hole in it large enough to fit over Mr. Frosty's head. This is the brim. Cut a narrow strip of board and felt. Roll the strip up and push into the brim. Stick in place with tape. Glue a black circle to the top of the hat.

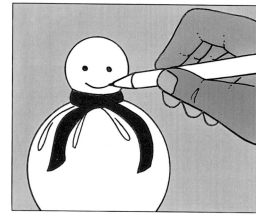

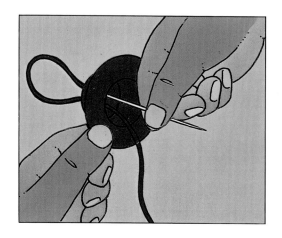

2 Draw a small circle about 1¾ inches in diameter on board. Cut it out and push it into the bottom of the white felt ball. Fill the ball with cotton and pull the ends of the thread tight and knot them securely. Glue the wooden bead to the top of the ball.

3 Cut a piece of ribbon to make a scarf and glue it in place. Use a black felt-tip pen to draw on Mr. Frosty's face, and stick on a piece of orange felt for his nose.

5 Thread a needle with black thread. Push the needle up through the hat and back down again to form a loop. Knot the ends of the thread together inside the hat. Glue the hat to the head.

STENCILED GLITTER CARDS

This form of stenciling uses glitter and glue to make the shapes instead of paint. The stencil is cut from firm paper and can be used again and again to print lots of cards or gift tags.

1 Draw your designs onto the firm paper. Objects with strong outlines, like candles, bells, and Christmas trees, work well.

YOU WILL NEED
Glitter in different colors
Glue stick
Firm paper for stencil
Colored cardboard
Scissors
Pencil and ruler
Newspaper

2 Push the scissor points into the center of your design, as shown. Carefully cut out the shape to make a "window" in the paper. This is the stencil.

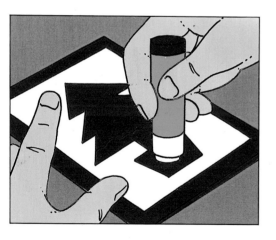

3 Cut the board into a rectangle. Place the stencil on top of the board and, holding it firmly in place, apply the glue to the cardboard through the cut-out shape.

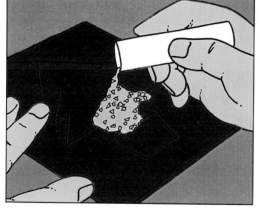

4 When all the cut-out area has been completely covered with glue, carefully lift off the stencil. While the glue is still wet, sprinkle the glitter onto it. Let it dry.

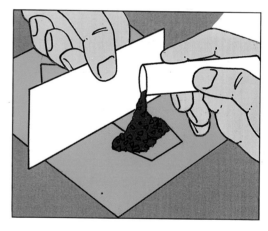

5 To make the glitter stripes, hold the straight edge of a spare piece of board over some of the glued surface, then shake on the glitter. Move the card and apply another color of glitter. Do this until the shape is covered. To finish, punch a hole through one corner of the card and thread some ribbon through it.

ROYAL CROWN

If you have to dress up for a Christmas fancy dress party, go as one of the three kings, wearing this fabulous crown. Decorate it with foil candy wrappers to look like jewels.

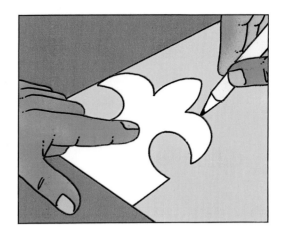

1 Using a pencil, trace the pattern on page 46. Turn the tracing paper over and lay it on a piece of scrap board. Rub firmly over the outline with a pencil. The image will appear on the board. Cut out the pattern. This is one section of the crown. Put the pattern on the gold board so that the straight edges match up. Draw around the shape.

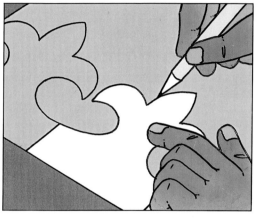

2 Move the pattern along and position it against the shape you have just drawn, as shown. Make sure the short sides match. Draw around the shape again. Repeat this until you have drawn around the pattern five times.

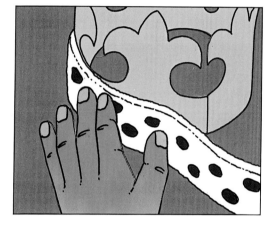

3 Carefully cut out the crown shape. Paint black dashes on the padding and let it dry. Curve the crown into shape, overlapping the edges. Tape the joint on the inside. Glue the padding to the lower edge of the crown, butting the edges together.

4 Cut squares from the colored foil and glue them onto the crown to look like jewels.

YOU WILL NEED
Lightweight gold cardboard
Colored foil candy wrappers
Cotton padding $26 \times 2\frac{1}{4}$ inches
Black paint and paintbrush
Masking tape
Scissors
Scrap cardboard
All-purpose glue
Tracing paper and pencil

MINI CARD WREATHS

Decorate your Christmas tree this year with these little wreaths made from cardboard, ribbons, and glittery sequins. The designs shown here are just a guide. You could also try decorating the wreaths with dried flowers, holly leaves, and berries.

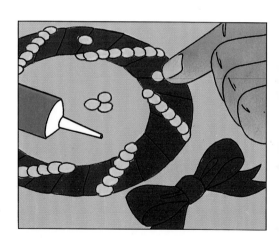

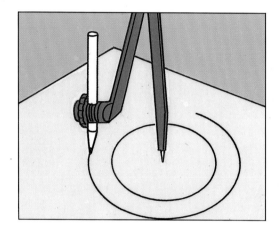

1 Using the compass, draw a circle about 2½ inches in diameter on the board. Leaving the point of the compass in the same position, draw a second circle about 1½ inches larger than the first. Carefully cut out the wreath.

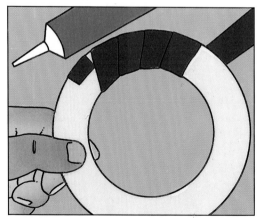

2 Dab some glue on the end of the ribbon and press it to the back of the wreath. When it has dried, twist the ribbon around and around the wreath so that all the board is covered. Glue the end of the ribbon to the back of the wreath.

3 Repeat with another trim, like sequin strips, this time forming it in much bigger loops. You might like to glue individual sequins on as well. Make a small bow from another colored ribbon and glue it to the top of the wreath.

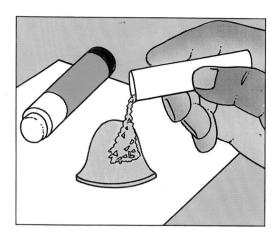

4 Cut out a bell shape from the gold board and lay it on spare paper. Cover the bell with glue and, while it is still wet, sprinkle glitter on top. Let it dry.

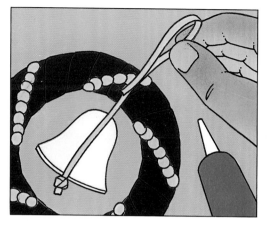

5 Cut a piece of cord about 6 inches long and tie a knot at one end. Glue the back of the bell to the end of the cord. Position the bell in the center of the wreath, taking the cord up at the back. Fold the cord back down into a loop and glue it behind the wreath.

YOU WILL NEED
Cardboard
Compass
Glitter
All-purpose glue
Scraps of gold cardboard
Ribbons, cords and sequins
Pencil
Scissors

PYRAMID GIFT BAGS

These pyramid-shaped gift bags are a great idea for making gifts look extra special at Christmas. Make small bags to hang on the Christmas tree, or larger ones to give as presents. Fill them to the top with candy or tiny gifts.

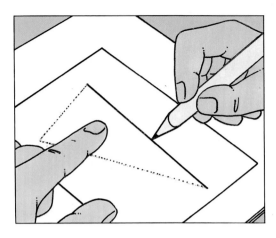

1 Using a pencil, trace either the large or the small triangle pattern on page 47. Turn the tracing over and lay it onto a piece of scrap cardboard. Rub firmly over the outline with a pencil. The pattern will appear on the board. Cut out the shape.

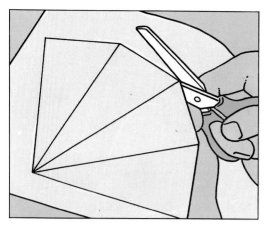

2 Lay the pattern onto the thin board and draw around it four times as shown. Keep the point in the same place each time and move the pattern along so that the long sides are edge-to-edge. Cut out the whole shape in one complete piece.

YOU WILL NEED

Thin cardboard
Giftwrap
Glue stick
Hole punch
Tracing paper and
  pencil
Scrap cardboard
Scissors
Ribbon or golden chain

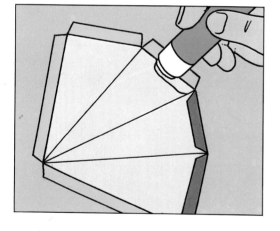

3 Coat the shape with glue and stick it to the wrong side of a sheet of giftwrap. Cut around the shape, leaving an extra 1 inch of giftwrap all around. Fold this over and glue to the cardboard.

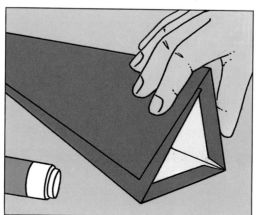

4 Fold the bag shape along three sides as shown. Glue two sections together to make a pyramid shape. Let it dry.

5 Punch a hole in the center of each section at the top. Thread ribbon or a golden chain through the holes to make handles. Tie the ends together.

PATTERNS

Some of the projects in this book are based on the patterns given on the following pages. To find out how to copy a pattern follow the step-by-step instructions given for each project.

You may want to make a pattern that you can keep to use again. To do this trace over the outline of the pattern with a pencil. Turn your tracing over and lay it onto a piece of thick cardboard. Rub firmly over the outline with a pencil. The image will appear on the board. Cut out the shape. If you keep this pattern in a safe place, you can use it time and time again.

CHRISTMAS STOCKING
Page 8

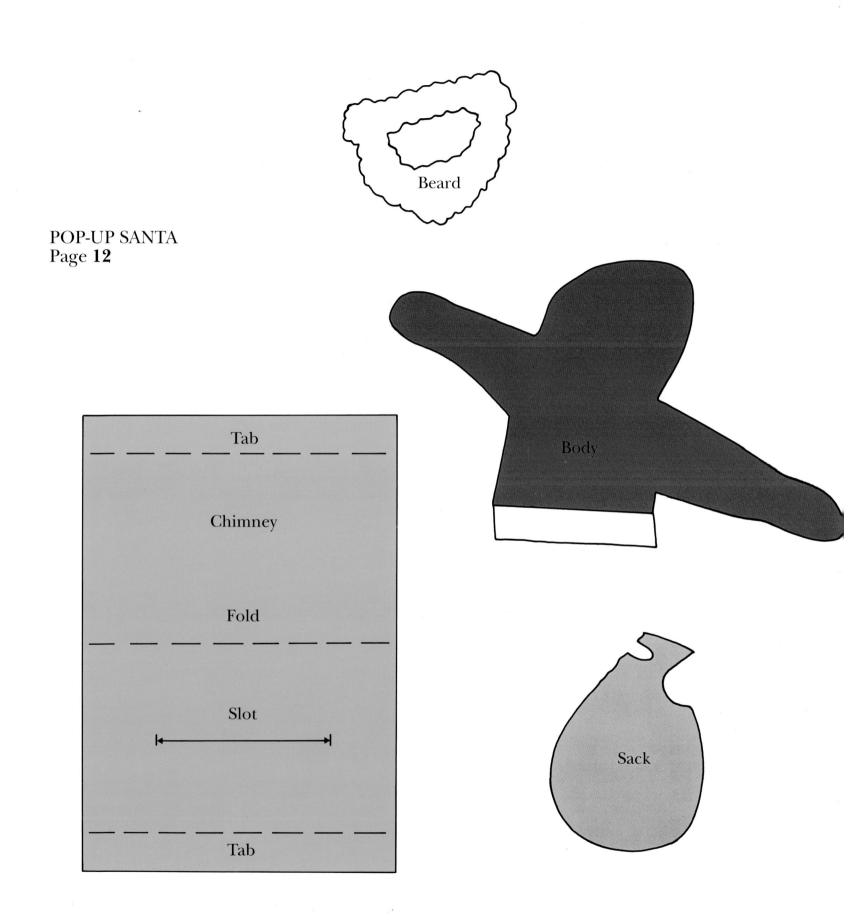

Beard

POP-UP SANTA
Page 12

Tab

Chimney

Fold

Slot

Tab

Body

Sack

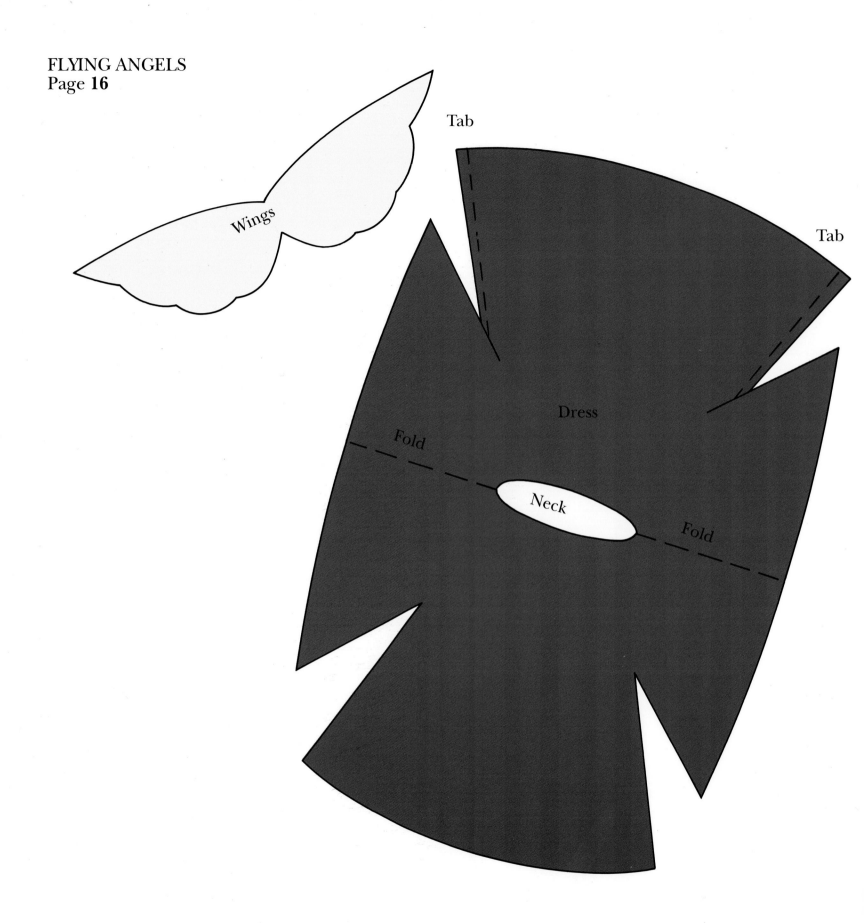

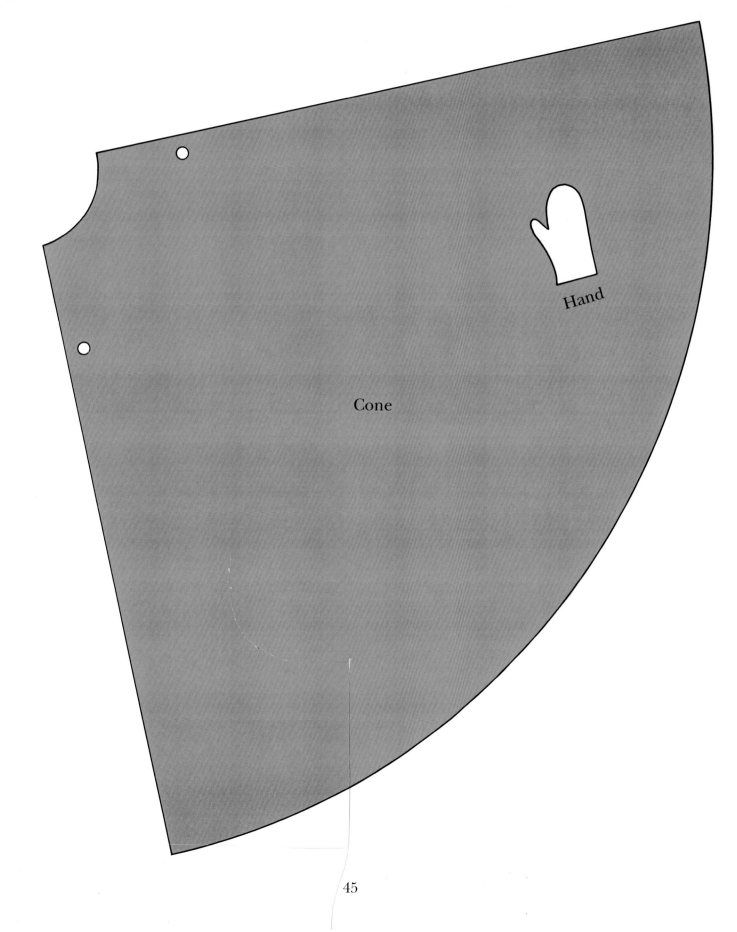

Hand

Cone

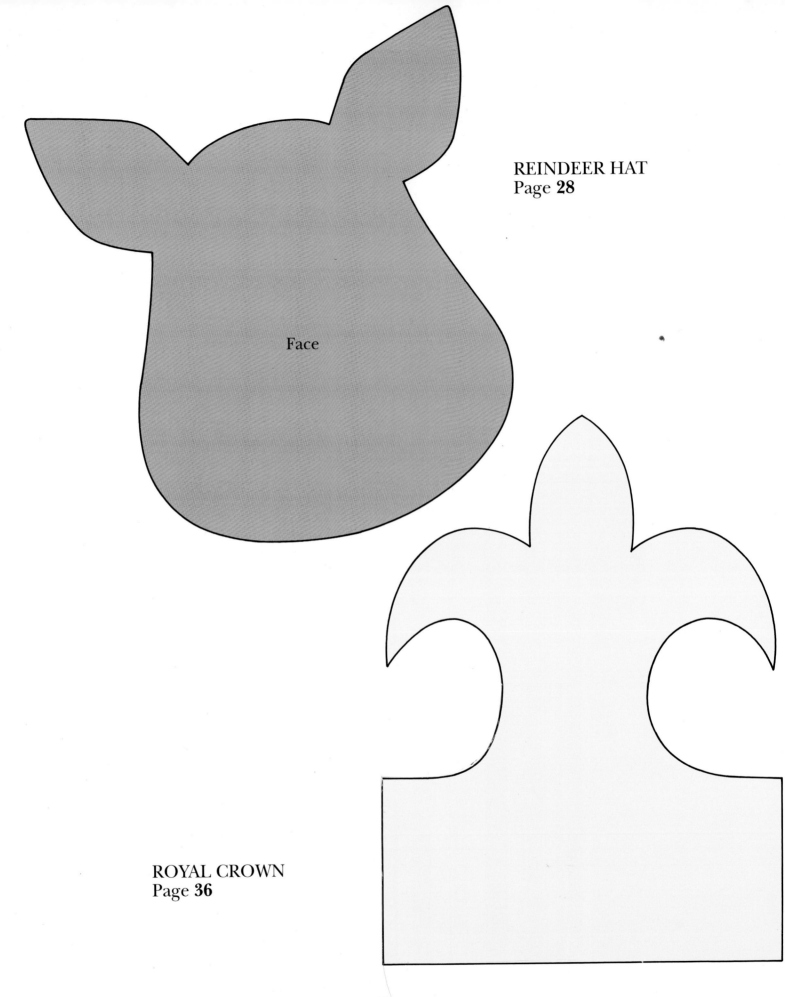

REINDEER HAT
Page **28**

Face

ROYAL CROWN
Page **36**

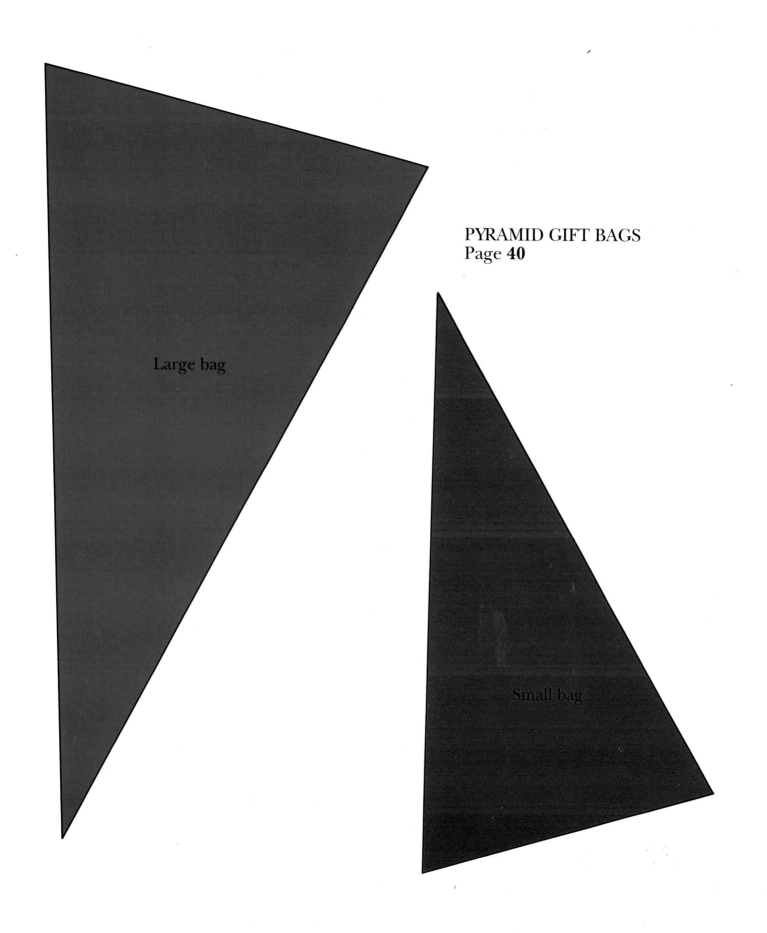

Large bag

PYRAMID GIFT BAGS
Page **40**

Small bag

INDEX

ACKNOWLEDGMENT
The publishers would like to
thank Hallmark Cards Ltd.,
Henley-on-Thames, Oxon,
United Kingdom, for their help
in compiling this book.